HOW SAFE IS YOUR CAR ?

An MOT handbook on mechanical safety

also covers
light vans and pick-ups

London: HMSO

Written and Designed by
Nick Lynch and Jon Starte

COMIND
Cambridge

ISBN 0 11 550964 X

Foreword

Road safety is important to us all. Drivers must share in this responsibility, which means driving carefully in a roadworthy vehicle and observing the requirements of the law.

For your vehicle to be safe and roadworthy, it must be regularly checked and maintained. Cars over three years old have to undergo the 'MOT' test every year, which is aimed at ensuring compliance with basic safety and legal requirements.

The practical, regular checks set out in this book are based on the 'MOT' test requirements. They are a handy guide to help you look after your car. Safe driving.

Christopher Chope MP
Minister for Roads and Traffic

Important notes

1. Regulations

This book is based on the regulations at the time of going to press. New regulations will come into force from time to time, or existing regulations may be amended.

For example, emission control regulations are expected to be introduced in 1991, and the regulations on tyre condition will change on 1 January 1992,

Information regarding the up-to-date regulations is available from MOT Testing Stations and from the Vehicle Inspectorate.

2. Tolerances

Because it is not possible to specify exact tolerances for wear, play, corrosion and so on, words such as 'excessive', 'serious' and 'too much' are sometimes used. If you feel unable to judge any item safely, seek expert advice.

INTRODUCTION

Why motorists should use this book

This book is produced by the Vehicle Inspectorate Executive Agency and sponsored by Norwich Union Insurance. Its purpose is to give motorists easy-to-follow advice on how to keep their vehicles safe, in good condition and within the legal requirements of the "MOT" Test.

It is not intended to interpret the law governing the "MOT" Test: that's a matter for the courts to determine.

This book does not replace the existing official MOT Testers Manual — Vehicle Testing used in the Test and also available from HMSO. Some testable items, such as brakes and headlamp-beam aim, can be difficult for you to check effectively without proper equipment..

This means that your vehicle can still fail, although you might have followed the procedures in this book to the letter. Remember that the "MOT" tester is specially trained and experienced: pass or fail is at his discretion.

If you feel you have a genuine grievance over a failure, you can appeal to the Vehicle Inspectorate's local District Office (see page 76).

While this book has been put together as a manual for those who want to check and/or prepare their vehicles for the "MOT" Test, it makes good sense to follow regularly the routines set out. Even if your vehicle is not due for an "MOT" Test, or perhaps not even within the scope of the scheme, it will pay you to carry out all these checks as part of your routine maintenance.

Put right any defects straight away: a minor defect can become dangerous if you neglect it.

If you have any doubts, don't hesitate to seek expert advice.

CONTENTS

ROUTINE

Follow these steps to check your car

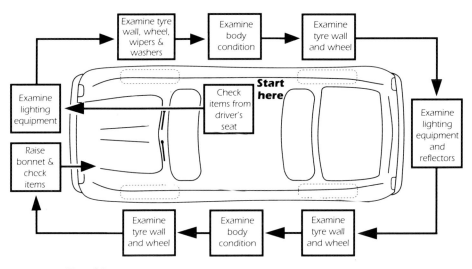

Topside

Warning

Before you check the underside, make
sure your car is safely jacked up and secured

With the front wheels in the straight
ahead position, check all relevant
underside items starting at offside front

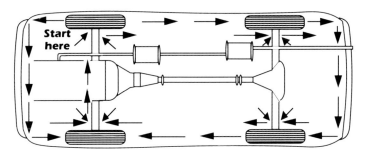

Underside

LIGHTS - 1

WHAT THE MOT REQUIRES	YOUR LIGHTS WHAT TO CHECK
The front lights **Your car must have:** 1. Two **front position** lamps (side lamps) 2. Two **dipped-beam** headlamps 3. Two **main-beam** headlamps Side lamps must give out either • white light, or • yellow light, if incorporated in headlamps with yellow lenses and switched separately These lamps must • be clean and in good working order • show a steady light • be equal distance from edge of car • be about equal height above the ground Cars used only in daylight do not require lamps. You must either remove **all** lamps or disconnect or mask them Cars first registered before 1 Jan 1931 are not required to have headlamps Cars requiring only one headlamp • have three wheels and first used before 1 Jan 1972 • weigh less than 400kg • are less than 1.3m wide Front Fog lamps or auxillary lamps are not included in the Test	**With ignition on, switch on lights and make sure that:** a. all lamps show a steady white or yellow light visible from a reasonable distance b. the light of any lamp is not affected when you switch on another lamp c. no lamp flickers when tapped d. each lamp is secure e. no lens is damaged or missing (for cracks see opposite page) f. all switches work correctly g. both matching lamps (eg both headlamps) show the same colour h. the aim of the headlamps complies with the relevant diagram on pages 6 and 7 i. matching pairs of lamps are in the correct position

2

Are your front lights safe ?

MAIN REASONS FOR FAILURE	REMARKS	ACTION	✓
1. Two symmetrically placed side lamps or headlamps NOT • showing a steady WHITE or YELLOW light • clean and in good working order	⚠ ⚠	Check Repair wiring/ Replace Recharge battery/ check positioning	
2. A lamp • does not light up as soon as it is switched on • is affected by the working of another lamp • flickers when you tap it	⚠ ⚠ ⚠	Check wiring and connections Repair/Replace	
3. A lens • missing • damaged (see below)	⚠	Repair/Replace	
4. A loose lamp	⚠ ⚠	Tighten	
5. A faulty switch	⚠ ⚠	Repair/Replace	

WARNING

 Extremely dangerous. DO NOT drive your car in this condition.
You will be breaking the law and risking your life and the lives of others.

 Very dangerous and may be illegal. Put right immediately.

 Could also be dangerous and illegal.

Note: A 'matched pair of lamps' means
• a pair of lamps the same height above ground
• one lamp on each side of car equal distance from edge of car
• both showing the same colour light

 ✗    ✓    ✗

Cracks in headlamp lenses (✓ acceptable ✗ not acceptable)

LIGHTS - 3

HOW TO TEST YOUR HEADLAMPS

You will need:

- A wall (such as the garage wall)
- A helpful friend
- A piece of chalk or other suitable marker

The test:

1. Check that your tyres are correctly inflated and the car is on level ground.

2. Draw on the wall

- a horizontal line about 2m long and at same height as centre of headlamp lens
- two vertical lines about 1m long each forming a cross with the horizontal line and the same distance apart as the headlamp centres
- another vertical line to form a cross on the horizontal line midway between the others

3. Position car so that

- it faces wall squarely and its centre line is in line with centre line marked on wall
- steering is straight
- headlamps lenses are 3.8 metres (12.5ft) from wall

4. Switch on the headlamps' 'main' and 'dipped' beams in turn. One of the beams will match one of the three images shown in the diagrams on pages 6 and 7.

5. Check that the boundaries of the beam image are not outside the limits given in the appropriate diagram.

4

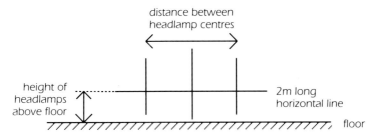

distance between headlamp centres

height of headlamps above floor

2m long horizontal line

floor

Drawing on wall

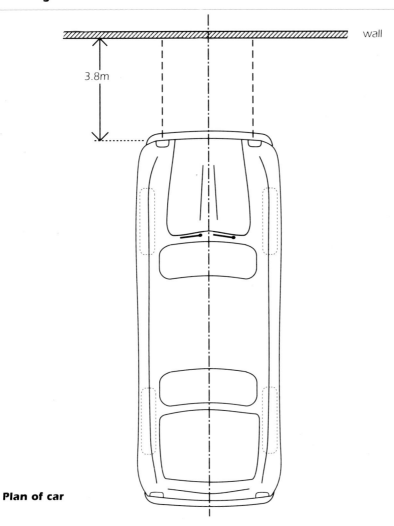

wall

3.8m

Plan of car

LIGHTS - 5

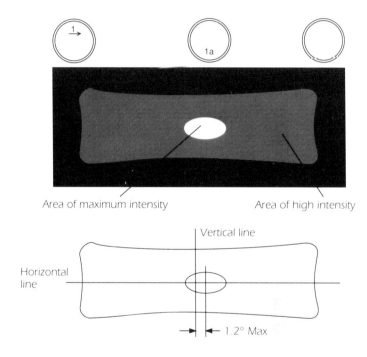

Area of maximum intensity   Area of high intensity

Vertical line

Horizontal line

1.2° Max

Diagram 1.
British American type headlamps checked on main (driving) beam

Note: 1° is approximately 66mm on the wall,
0.5° is 33mm, and so on.

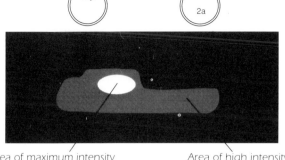

Area of maximum intensity   Area of high intensity

Vertical line

Horizontal line   0.25° Max

Diagram 2.
British American type headlamps checked on dipped beam

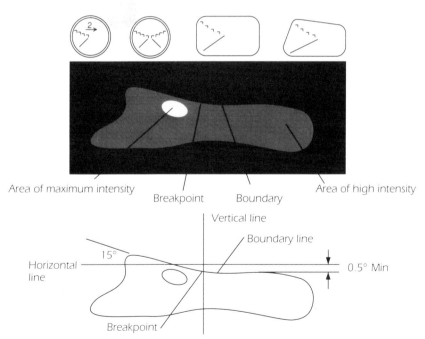

Area of maximum intensity   Breakpoint   Boundary   Area of high intensity

Vertical line

Boundary line

Horizontal line   15°   0.5° Min

Breakpoint

Diagram 3.
European type headlamps checked on dipped beam

Note: 1° is approximately 66mm on the wall,
0.5° is 33mm, and so on.

LIGHTS - 7

WHAT THE MOT REQUIRES	HOW TO CHECK YOUR LIGHTS
The rear lights **Your car must have:** 1. Two **rear position lamps** which give out a steady RED light 2. Two **stop lamps** which give out a steady red light when the footbrake is applied These lamps must • be clean and in good working order • show a steady light • be equal distance from centre of car • be about the same height above the ground Cars used only in daylight do not require lamps. You must either remove **all** lamps or disconnect or mask them Cars not required to have stop lamps are those • first used before 1 Jan 1936 • with a maximum speed not exceeding 15mph (by Law or power) • without electrically operated lighting equipment Cars only required to have one stop lamp are those • first used after 1 Jan 1936 and before 1 Jan 1971 Rear fog lamps or auxilliary lamps are not included in the Test	**Switch on lights and make sure that:** a. rear position lamps show a steady RED light b. when footbrake is applied the RED stop lamps light up c. no lamp is affected by the operation of any other lamp d. no lamp flickers when tapped e. each lamp is secure f. no lens is damaged or missing (for cracks, see page 3) g. all switches work correctly h. matching pairs of lamps are in the correct position

Are your rear lights safe ?

MAIN REASONS FOR FAILURE	REMARKS	ACTION	✓
1. Stop lamps do not show a steady RED light when you apply footbrake	⚠ ⚠ ⚠	Check bulb Check wiring Check switch Repair/Replace	
2. Stop lamps do not stay steadily lit while you keep brakes applied	⚠ ⚠	Check wiring Repair/Replace	
3. Stop lamps remain on while brakes are not being applied	⚠	Check wiring Check switch Repair/Replace	
4. Rear position lamps do not show a steady red light	⚠ ⚠	Check bulb Check wiring Repair/Replace	
5. A stop or rear position lamp • does not light up as soon as it is switched on • is affected by the working of another lamp • flickers when you tap it	⚠ ⚠ ⚠	Check wiring and connections Repair/Replace	
6. A lens • missing • damaged (see page 3)	⚠	Replace	
7. A loose lamp	⚠ ⚠	Tighten	
8. A faulty switch	⚠ ⚠	Repair/Replace	

WARNING

 Extremely dangerous. DO NOT drive your car in this condition.
You will be breaking the law and risking your life and the lives of others.

 Very dangerous and may be illegal. Put right immediately.

Could also be dangerous and illegal.

LIGHTS - 9

WHAT THE MOT REQUIRES	HOW TO CHECK YOUR INDICATORS
The indicators **Your car must have:** 1. two **direction indicators** which • show an **amber** light to the front • show an **amber** light to the rear • flash between 1-2 times per second (with engine running, if necessary) • can be seen by driver from normal driving position (if not, an audible or visible telltale must be fitted and work correctly) • are clean and in good working order Cars first used before 1 Jan 1936, and those that cannot exceed 15 mph do not require direction indicators. For cars fitted with semaphore arms they should • move freely and not stick • be illuminated amber on both sides • be seen by driver from a normal driving position (if not, an audible or visible telltale must be fitted and work correctly) Cars first used before 1 Sept 1965 may have indicators which show a **white** light to the front and a **red** light to the rear. However, the light must be **amber** if it can be seen from front and rear.	**Switch on direction indicators in turn and make sure that:** a. light is correct colour b. they flash 1-2 times a second c. intensity is reasonable d. telltale is working correctly if indicators are not visible from driving position e. no lamp affects the working of any other lamp f. no lamp flickers when tapped g. no lamp is loose h. no lens is damaged or missing i. switches work correctly

LIGHTS - 10

Are your indicators working properly ?

MAIN REASONS FOR FAILURE	REMARKS	ACTION	✓
1. An indicator missing or can't be seen	⚠ ⚠	Repair/Replace	
2. An indicator • not showing the correct colour • not visible from a reasonable distance	⚠ ⚠	Repair/Replace	
3. An indicator • not working • not flashing at the correct rate • affected by another lamp	⚠ ⚠	Check wiring Repair/Replace	
4. A light • does not light up as soon as it is switched on • is affected by the working of another lamp • flickers when you tap it	⚠ ⚠	Check switch Check wiring and connections Repair/Replace	
5. A lens, • missing • damaged • not doing its job	⚠	Repair/Replace	
6. A loose lamp	⚠ ⚠	Tighten	
7. A faulty switch	⚠	Repair/Replace	

WARNING

⚠ ⚠ Very dangerous and may be illegal. Put right immediately.

⚠ Could also be dangerous and illegal.

11

LIGHTS - 11

Are your reflectors in good condition ?

WHAT THE MOT REQUIRES	HOW TO CHECK YOUR REFLECTORS
The rear reflectors **Your car must have:** 1. Two **rear retro reflectors** which are • unobscured • fitted squarely to face the rear • equal distance from edge of car, one on each side at rear • clean Cars used only during the day which • have no lamps • have disconnected or masked lamps do not need reflectors Extra reflectors are not included in the Test **NOTE: Reflective tape is NOT acceptable in place of a reflector**	**Check you have clean RED rear reflectors** a. Examine their condition, security and position

Are your reflectors in good condition ?

MAIN REASONS FOR FAILURE	REMARKS	ACTION	✓
1. A rear reflector • missing • obscured • incorrectly positioned • not red	⚠ ⚠ ⚠	Repair/Replace	
2. A reflector • damaged • not doing its job	⚠ ⚠	Repair/Replace	
3. A loose reflector	⚠	Tighten	

WARNING

⚠ ⚠ ⚠   Extremely dangerous. DO NOT drive your car in this condition. You will be breaking the law and risking your life and the lives of others.

 Very dangerous and may be illegal. Put right immediately.

 Could also be dangerous and illegal.

STEERING - 1

Checks from driver's seat

Is your car's steering safe ?

WHAT THE MOT REQUIRES	HOW TO CHECK YOUR STEERING
The steering controls The condition of the STEERING must not cause danger to any person in the car or on the road The STEERING must be in good and efficient working order and be properly adjusted	Release steering lock, if car has one a. Check that any mechanism for adjusting steering column is fully locked b. Turn steering wheel from side to side while checking for excessive movement due to wear c. Pull and push steering wheel while checking for movement in centre of column d. Check that steering column is securely mounted to body of car e. Check steering wheel hub, spokes and rim for fractures or loose spokes

Is your car's steering safe ?

MAIN REASONS FOR FAILURE	REMARKS	ACTION	✓
1. Any relative movement between steering wheel and steering column	⚠ ⚠	Tighten/Replace	
2. Any abnormal movement indicating column top bearing is • excessively worn	⚠	Replace	
3. Any movement up and down in the centre of steering column due to • worn steering box • deteriorated flexible coupling • worn upper column bearings	⚠ ⚠	Tighten/Repair Replace	
4. Any movement due to • insecure or • fractured top mounting bracket	⚠ ⚠ ⚠	Tighten/Repair Replace	
5. The spoke, hub or rim of steering wheel is • loose or • fractured	⚠ ⚠ ⚠	Repair/Replace	

WARNING

 Extremely dangerous. DO NOT drive your car in this condition. You will be breaking the law and risking your life and the lives of others.

 Very dangerous and may be illegal. Put right immediately.

 Could also be dangerous and illegal.

STEERING - 3

Is your car's steering safe ?

WHAT THE MOT REQUIRES	HOW TO CHECK YOUR STEERING
The steering system The condition of the STEERING must not cause danger to any person in the car or on the road The STEERING must be in good and efficient working order and be correctly adjusted	Put the wheels in a straight ahead position supporting the weight of the car a. Check there is no excess movement of steering wheel when drop arm or steering rod is felt or seen to move slightly b. Get a friend to turn steering wheel from side to side, while you check for Movement between • chassis and steering box or rack • connecting joints in the mechanical linkage Insecure • parts of steering box or rack • balljoints • all nuts and locking devices • attachment of steering damper Damage, corrosion or fracture of • area around steering box, rack or idler • steering damper body or cover Excess • fluid leakage from a steering damper • wear in pivot point, ball joint and any other joints The condition of drive shaft universal joint couplings (front wheel drive cars only)

Is your car's steering safe ?

MAIN REASONS FOR FAILURE	REMARKS	ACTION	✓
1. Steering wheel • stiff • too much free play	⚠ ⚠ ⚠	Adjust/Replace	
2. Too much movement between mechanical linkage and connecting joints	⚠ ⚠ ⚠	Tighten/Replace	
3. Insecure • track rod end • drag link end • ball pin shank • steering box/rack • pinion assembly • bolt • retaining device • locking device • steering damper • drive shaft constant velocity joint • universal joint coupling • U bolt securing a joint bearing	⚠ ⚠ ⚠	Tighten/Replace	
4. Damaged, corroded, or fractured • bushing material • flexible rubber • steering component • sector shaft • damper body • steering box/rack • pinion housing bolt • fabric universal coupling unit	⚠ ⚠ ⚠	Repair/Replace	
5. Fluid leakage from a steering damper indicating failure	⚠ ⚠	Repair/Replace	
6. The loadbearing member and/or panel within 30cm of steering box, rack and pinion housing, or mounting point of any part of steering assembly is • excessively corroded • deformed, or • fractured	⚠ ⚠	Repair/Replace	

WARNING

 Extremely dangerous. DO NOT drive your car in this condition. You will be breaking the law and risking your life and the lives of others.

Very dangerous and may be illegal. Put right immediately.

STEERING - 5

Is your car's steering safe ?

WHAT THE MOT REQUIRES	HOW TO CHECK YOUR POWER STEERING
Power steering The condition of the STEERING must not cause danger to any person in the car or on the road The STEERING must be in good and efficient working order and be correctly adjusted	Select neutral gear. Put parking brake on and start engine. Turn steering wheel from side to side and check a. That all parts similar to normal steering mechanism are correct b. That no hydraulic fluid hose or union is leaking (Switch off engine) c. The condition of power steering pump drive and security of pump mounting d. For power assistance

Is your car's steering safe ?

MAIN REASONS FOR FAILURE	REMARKS	ACTION	✓
1. Power steering does not operate correctly	⚠ ⚠ ⚠	Adjust/Replace	
2. Any part is insecure	⚠ ⚠ ⚠	Adjust/Replace	
3. Excessive play in a power steering mechanism joint	⚠ ⚠	Tighten	
4. Excessive deterioration of any bushing material	⚠ ⚠	Replace	
5. Fluid leak or damaged hose	⚠ ⚠ ⚠	Repair/Replace	

WARNING

 Extremely dangerous. DO NOT drive your car in this condition.
You will be breaking the law and risking your life and the lives of others.

 Very dangerous and may be illegal. Put right immediately.

SUSPENSION & WHEEL BEARINGS - 1

Are your car's front wheel bearings in good condition ?

WHAT THE MOT REQUIRES	HOW TO CHECK YOUR BEARINGS

The front wheel bearings
 	
The condition of the BEARINGS must not cause danger to any person in the car or on the road
 	
The BEARINGS must be maintained in good and efficient working order
 	
Note
Rear wheel bearings are not included in the Test
	a. Preferably with the car over a pit or on a raised hoist, jack up front wheels (for jacking positions, see pages 24-28)
	
	b. While wheels are being jacked up, look for movement in inner wishbone bearings
	
	c. When car is jacked up, check for
	
	• roughness in bearings when spinning the wheel
	
	• tightness or excessive play when the wheel is stationary. Do this with wheel in at least two positions
	
	d. For front wheel drive cars,
	• put gear in neutral
	• spin wheels at each steering lock and check
	   - condition of gaiters, and
	   - front wheel drive shafts
	    for straightness and damage

SUSPENSION & WHEEL BEARINGS - 2

Are your car's front wheel bearings in good condition ?

MAIN REASONS FOR FAILURE	REMARKS	ACTION	✓
1. A wishbone bearing or pin • worn • corroded • bent	⚠	Replace	
2. A flexible rubber bush seriously deteriorated	⚠	Replace	
3. A wheel bearing • rough • tight • has excessive play, or • has not enough clearance	⚠	Adjust/Replace	
4. A universal joint gaiter • split • missing • insecurely mounted	⚠ ⚠	Adjust/Replace	
5. A damaged or bent • shaft • locking device	⚠ ⚠	Tighten/Lock	
6. A locking device is missing or defective	⚠ ⚠	Repair/Replace	

WARNING

 Very dangerous and may be illegal. Put right immediately.

⚠ Could also be dangerous and illegal.

SUSPENSION - 1

Is your car's suspension in good condition ?

WHAT THE MOT REQUIRES	HOW TO CHECK YOUR SUSPENSION
All suspension types The condition of the SUSPENSION must not cause danger to any person in the car or on the road The SUSPENSION must be in good and efficient working order and be correctly adjusted	a. Place front wheels on a device or a surface which enables wheels to turn without much resistance b. While turning wheels from lock to lock,, check • the flexible hoses are not fouling any moving part • lockstops for security and correct adjustment • condition and security of steering rack gaiters • there is no tightness or roughness c. Examine condition of • wishbones • inner bearings • track control arms • suspension radius rods • mounting bushes • thrust washers or bearings • suspension spring d. Correct mounting of • suspension spring • displacer • bellows

Is your car's suspension in good condition ?

MAIN REASONS FOR FAILURE	REMARKS	ACTION	✓
1. Any part of the steering mechanism • interfering with fixed part of car • too tight • insecure • rough in operation	⚠ ⚠	Adjust/Replace	
2. A lock stop • incorrectly adjusted • insecure • loose • damaged	⚠ ⚠	Adjust/Replace	
3. A steering rack gaiter • insecure • split • missing	⚠ ⚠	Replace	
4. A metal or flexible brake hose is • stretched • twisted • seriously damaged by fouling	⚠ ⚠ ⚠	Replace	
5. Excessive wear in a . • pin • wishbone bearing or seriously deteriorated flexible bush	⚠ ⚠	Replace	
6. A wishbone, track control arm, or radius rod is fractured or • distorted • insecure • excessively corroded	⚠ ⚠ ⚠ ⚠ ⚠	Replace	
7. A seriously deteriorated • radius arm • flexible bearing • thrust washer or bearing	⚠ ⚠	Replace	
8. A radius arm nut insecurely locked	⚠ ⚠	Lock/Replace	

WARNING

⚠ ⚠ ⚠ Extremely dangerous. DO NOT drive your car in this condition.
You will be breaking the law and risking your life and the lives of others.

⚠ ⚠ Very dangerous and may be illegal. Put right immediately.

SUSPENSION - 3

Is your car's suspension in good condition ?

WHAT THE MOT REQUIRES	HOW TO CHECK YOUR SUSPENSION
Suspension types 1 & 2 (See Figures 1 & 2 below) The condition of the SUSPENSION must not cause danger to any person in the car or on the road The SUSPENSION must be in good and efficient working order and be correctly adjusted	a. Jack up front suspension so that wheels are clear of the ground b. Ask a friend to • hold wheel at top and bottom (see Figure 5 on page 27), and • rock wheel backwards and forwards Check for movement • between kingpin and its bushes or in axle boss • between wishbone outer suspension ball joints and their housings • in upper inner wishbone bearings c. With a bar under each front roadwheel, try to lift wheel and check for movement between • stub axle yoke and its housing at the thrust bearing • suspension ball joints and their housing d. Check beam axles, wishbones and stub axles for damage and distortion e. Examine condition of chassis frame and body shell structure around suspension mounting points for fractures, corrosion and distortion

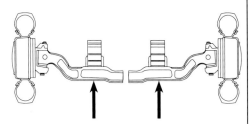

Figure 1. Suspension type 1
Jack up at points indicated by arrows*

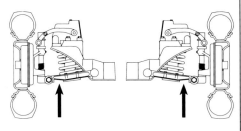

Figure 2. Suspension type 2
Jack up at points indicated by arrows*

*Use suitable jacks. Your car jack may not be the right type for this job.

Is your car's suspension in good condition ?

MAIN REASONS FOR FAILURE	REMARKS	ACTION	✓
1. A kingpin is loose in its • mounting boss or • stub axle bush	⚠️⚠️⚠️	Tighten/Replace	
2. A kingpin retaining device is loose or missing	⚠️⚠️⚠️	Tighten/Replace	
3. Excessive wear in • suspension swivel pin • suspension ball joint • wishbone bearing or flexible bush	⚠️⚠️	Replace	
4. Excessive lift between stub axle and axle housing	⚠️⚠️	Adjust/Repair	
5. Excessive play caused by wear in a ball joint	⚠️⚠️	Replace	
6. A distorted axle beam or component	⚠️⚠️	Replace	
7. A wishbone arm is fractured or • excessively corroded • distorted	⚠️⚠️⚠️ ⚠️⚠️	Replace	
8. The loadbearing member and/or panel within 30cm of the mounting point for the suspension is • excessively corroded • deformed　　• fractured	⚠️⚠️	Repair/Replace	

SUSPENSION - 5

Is your car's suspension in good condition ?

	HOW TO CHECK YOUR SUSPENSION
Suspension types 3 & 3a (See Figures 3 & 4 below) The condition of the SUSPENSION must not cause danger to any person in the car or on the road The SUSPENSION must be in good and efficient working order and be correctly adjusted	a. Place the front wheels on a device or a surface which enables the wheels to turn without much resistance b. Shake wheel vigorously (see Figures 6 & 7 on opposite page) and check for • play between ball and its housing in suspension ball joint • a seriously worn pin or bush in an inner wishbone bearing

Figure 3. Suspension type 3
Jack up at points indicated by arrows*

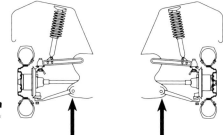

Figure 4. Suspension type 3a
Jack up at points indicated by arrows*

*Use suitable jacks. Your car jack may not be the right type for this job.

Is your car's suspension in good condition ?

MAIN REASONS FOR FAILURE	REMARKS	ACTION	✓
1. Suspension ball joint seriously worn	⚠️ ⚠️ ⚠️	Replace	
2. A ball joint nut/securing nut is • loose • not locked	⚠️ ⚠️	Tighten/Lock	
3. A seriously worn • pin • bush • inner wishbone bearing	⚠️ ⚠️ ⚠️	Replace	

WARNING

⚠️ ⚠️ ⚠️   Extremely dangerous. DO NOT drive your car in this condition.
You will be breaking the law and risking your life and the lives of others.

⚠️ ⚠️   Very dangerous and may be illegal. Put right immediately.

Top

Bottom

Figure 5.
Hands at 6 o'clock
and 12 o'clock positions
(top and bottom of wheel)
Rock wheel backwards and for-
wards.

Front   Rear

Figure 6.
Both hands at 12 o'clock position
(top of wheel). Push and pull wheel.

Front   Rear

Figure 7.
Hands at 3 o'clock
and 9 o'clock positions (each
side of wheel). Swivel wheel in
short, sharp steering actions.

27

SUSPENSION - 7

Is your car's suspension in good condition ?

WHAT THE MOT REQUIRES	HOW TO CHECK YOUR SUSPENSION

Suspension type 4
(See Figure 8 below)
 	
The condition of the SUSPENSION must not cause danger to any person in the car or on the road
 	
The SUSPENSION must be in good and efficient working order and be correctly adjusted
	a. Place front wheels on a device or surface which enables wheels to turn without much resistance
	
	b. Place both hands on top of wheel and push and pull wheel (See Figure 6 on page 27)
	
	c. Check for
	
	• wear in a shock absorber strut and/or bush
	
	• in rod
	
	• movement at upper support bearing
	
	• leak of fluid from gland
	
	• corrosion or damage to strut casing
	
	• condition of bonding between metal and flexible material in strut upper-support bearing
	
	d. Hold wheel at 3 o'clock and 9 o'clock positions (see Figure7 on page 27). Swivel wheel in short, sharp steering actions and check for movement of
	    - strut lower ball joint
	    - track control arm inner bushes
	
	e. Check each coil rod spring for
	• correct mounting
	• damage

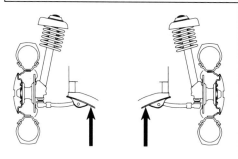

Figure 8. Suspension type 4
Jack up at points indicated by arrows*

*Use suitable jacks. Your car jack may not be the right type for this job.

Is your car's suspension in good condition ?

MAIN REASONS FOR FAILURE	REMARKS	ACTION	✓
1. A suspension strut and/or bush is worn	⚠ ⚠	Replace	
2. Shock absorber gland leaking fluid	⚠ ⚠	Repair/Replace	
3. A strut upper bearing assembly is • rough • stiff • has too much free play	⚠ ⚠	Adjust/Replace	
4. A strut casing has • damage • excessive corrosion	⚠ ⚠	Replace	
5. Excessive deterioration in bonding between metal and flexible material of an upper support bearing	⚠ ⚠	Replace	
6. A lock nut in upper support bearing • loose • insecurely locked	⚠ ⚠	Tighten/Lock	
7. Excessive deterioration in bonding or flexible material of • track control arm • radius member bush • radius member mounting	⚠ ⚠	Replace	
8. Excessive wear in a strut lower ball joint	⚠ ⚠ ⚠	Repair/Replace	
9. A ball joint or assembly cover nut is • loose • insecurely locked	⚠ ⚠ ⚠	Tighten/Lock	
10. The loadbearing member and/or panel within 30cm of the mounting point for the suspension is • excessively corroded • deformed • fractured	⚠ ⚠	Repair/Replace	

WARNING

⚠ ⚠ ⚠ Extremely dangerous. DO NOT drive your car in this condition.
You will be breaking the law and risking your life and the lives of others.

⚠ ⚠ Very dangerous and may be illegal. Put right immediately.

SUSPENSION ASSEMBLIES - 1

Is your car's sub-frame in good condition ?

WHAT THE MOT REQUIRES	HOW TO CHECK YOUR SUB-FRAME
The sub-frame The condition of the SUB-FRAME must not cause danger to any person in the car or on the road	a. Examine the condition of sub-frame b. Check mountings for • fractures • excessive corrosion • insecurity • deterioration

SUSPENSION ASSEMBLIES - 2

Is your car's sub-frame in good condition ?

MAIN REASONS FOR FAILURE	REMARKS	ACTION	✓
1. A sub-frame is badly • distorted • fractured • corroded • repaired	⚠ ⚠ ⚠ ⚠ ⚠ ⚠ ⚠ ⚠ ⚠	Repair/Replace	
2. An insecurely locked or defective mounting	⚠ ⚠	Lock/Replace	
3. A badly deteriorated flexible mounting	⚠	Replace	
4. The loadbearing member and/or panel within 30cm of the mounting point for the sub-frame is • excessively corroded • deformed • fractured	⚠ ⚠	Repair/Replace	

WARNING

 Extremely dangerous. DO NOT drive your car in this condition. You will be breaking the law and risking your life and the lives of others.

 Very dangerous and may be illegal. Put right immediately.

Could also be dangerous and illegal.

SUSPENSION ASSEMBLIES - 3

Is your car's suspension assembly in good condition ?

WHAT THE MOT REQUIRES	HOW TO CHECK YOUR SUSPENSION
The coil spring or displacer units The condition of the ASSEMBLY must not cause danger to any person in the car or on the road The ASSEMBLY must be in good and efficient working order	**How to check the condition of your coil spring and displacer units** a. Check each coil spring and displacer unit for • correct mounting • damage b. Check car's structure near mounting point for • fractures • excessive corrosion • distortion c. Examine any interconnecting pipes between displacer units

SUSPENSION ASSEMBLIES - 4

Is your car's suspension assembly in good condition ?

MAIN REASONS FOR FAILURE	REMARKS	ACTION	✓
1. A coil spring • incomplete • fractured • seriously reduced cross section due to corrosion or wear	⚠⚠⚠	Replace	
2. A coil spring or displacer unit incorrectly seated	⚠⚠⚠	Adjust	
3. Inadequate clearance of the axle or suspension with the bump stop or chassis	⚠	Replace/Repair	
4. Interconnecting pipes between displacer units are • damaged • excessively corroded • insecure • leaking	⚠⚠	Replace	
5. The loadbearing member and/or panel within 30cm of the mounting point for the spring is • excessively corroded • deformed • fractured	⚠⚠	Repair/Replace	

WARNING

 Extremely dangerous. DO NOT drive your car in this condition.
You will be breaking the law and risking your life and the lives of others.

 Very dangerous and may be illegal. Put right immediately.

 Could also be dangerous and illegal.

SUSPENSION ASSEMBLIES - 5

Is your car's suspension assembly in good condition ?

WHAT THE MOT REQUIRES	HOW TO CHECK YOUR LEAF SPRINGS
The leaf spring The condition of the ASSEMBLY must not cause danger to any person in the car or on the road The ASSEMBLY must be in good and efficient working order	a. Check each leaf spring for • fractures • displaced leaves • deformation b. Check that each spring is fitted so that • the axle is correctly located • it is secured to the axle c. Check • spring anchor bracket • spring shackle bracket • associated pins and bushes for • wear • security • adequate locking • side play d. Check car's structure within 30cm of any spring mounting for • fractures • excessive corrosion • distortion

SUSPENSION ASSEMBLIES - 6

Is your car's suspension assembly in good condition ?

MAIN REASONS FOR FAILURE	REMARKS	ACTION	✓
1. A leaf in a spring is • incomplete • fractured • splayed excessively	⚠⚠⚠	Repair/Replace	
2. Not enough clearance of the axle or suspension with the bump stop or chassis	⚠	Repair/Replace	
3. A broken centre bolt	⚠⚠⚠	Replace	
4. Spring incorrectly fitted so the axle is incorrectly located	⚠⚠⚠	Adjust/Replace	
5. A loose securing bolt or plate	⚠ ⚠	Adjust/Replace	
6. A defective spring eye	⚠ ⚠	Replace	
7. An anchor pin and bush • loose in its bracket • insecure • excessively worn • missing	⚠⚠⚠	Adjust/Replace	
8. A shackle pin and/or bush • loose in its bracket • insecure • excessively worn • missing	⚠ ⚠	Adjust/Replace	
9. The loadbearing member and/or panel within 30cm of the mounting point for the spring is • excessively corroded • deformed • fractured	⚠⚠⚠	Repair/Replace	

WARNING

 Extremely dangerous. DO NOT drive your car in this condition.
You will be breaking the law and risking your life and the lives of others.

 Very dangerous and may be illegal. Put right immediately.

 Could also be dangerous and illegal.

SUSPENSION ASSEMBLIES - 7

Is your car's suspension assembly in good condition ?

WHAT THE MOT REQUIRES	HOW TO CHECK YOUR SUSPENSION
Radius arms, links and tie bars The condition of the ASSEMBLY must not cause danger to any person in the car or on the road The ASSEMBLY must be in good and efficient working order and be correctly adjusted	**How to check the condition of radius arms, links and tie bars.** a. Check each radius arm, link and tie bar for • fractures • distortion • excessive corrosion b. Check mountings for • wear • security c. On vehicles which have a drive shaft which forms part of suspension, check for • distortion • damage • serious corrosion On these vehicles check universal joint bearings for wear, and flanges and bolts for security d. Check car's structure and panel within 30cm of arm/ link mountings for • fractures • excessive corrosion • distortion

SUSPENSION ASSEMBLIES - 8

Is your car's suspension assembly in good condition ?

MAIN REASONS FOR FAILURE	REMARKS	ACTION	✓
1. A radius arm or locating link • distorted • fractured • excessively corroded	⚠⚠⚠	Replace	
2. Excessive wear in a radius arm or locating link bush or bearing	⚠ ⚠	Replace	
3. A radius arm or locating link mounting or pin • insecure • not properly locked	⚠ ⚠	Tighten/Lock	
4. Serious deterioration of bonding or flexible material of a radius arm or link	⚠ ⚠	Repair/Replace	
5. A drive shaft • distorted • damaged • excessively corroded	⚠ ⚠	Replace	
6. Excessively worn universal joint bearing	⚠ ⚠	Replace	
7. An incorrectly seated universal joint flange	⚠ ⚠	Adjust/Replace	
8. A loose flange bolt	⚠ ⚠	Tighten/Lock	
9. The loadbearing member and/or panel within 30cm of the mounting point for radius arm or locating link is • excessively corroded • deformed • fractured	⚠⚠⚠	Repair/Replace	

WARNING

 Extremely dangerous. DO NOT drive your car in this condition.
You will be breaking the law and risking your life and the lives of others.

 Very dangerous and may be illegal. Put right immediately.

SUSPENSION ASSEMBLIES - 9

Is your car's suspension assembly in good condition ?

WHAT THE MOT REQUIRES	HOW TO CHECK YOUR TORSION BARS
Torsion bars The condition of the ASSEMBLY must not cause danger to any person in the car or on the road The ASSEMBLY must be in good and efficient working order and be correctly adjusted	a. Check each torsion bar for • fractures • distortion • excessive corrosion • pitting • free play where torsion bar is connected to suspension arm, guide or wishbone b. Check security of torsion bar abutment screw assembly to the body structure of the car c. Check the car's structure within 30cm of the mounting point of a torsion bar attachment for • fractures • excessive corrosion • distortion

SUSPENSION ASSEMBLIES - 10

Is your car's suspension assembly in good condition ?

MAIN REASONS FOR FAILURE	REMARKS	ACTION	✓
1. A torsion bar • distorted • fractured • excessively corroded	⚠⚠⚠	Replace	
2. Excessive free play where torsion bar is connected to suspension arm or wishbone	⚠ ⚠	Replace	
3. A torsion bar abutment • damaged • not properly locked	⚠ ⚠	Tighten/Replace	
4. Not enough clearance of axle or suspension with bump stop or chassis	⚠	Adjust/Replace	
5. The loadbearing member and/or panel within 30cm of the mounting point for a torsion bar attachment is • excessively corroded • deformed • fractured	⚠⚠⚠	Repair/Replace	

WARNING

 Extremely dangerous. DO NOT drive your car in this condition.
You will be breaking the law and risking your life and the lives of others.

 Very dangerous and may be illegal. Put right immediately.

 Could also be dangerous and illegal.

SUSPENSION ASSEMBLIES - 11

Is your car's suspension assembly in good condition ?

WHAT THE MOT REQUIRES	HOW TO CHECK YOUR ANTI-ROLL BARS
Anti-roll bar The condition of the ASSEMBLY must not cause danger to any person in the car or on the road The ASSEMBLY must be in good and efficient working order and be correctly adjusted	a. Check each anti-roll bar for • fractures • distortion • excessive corrosion • security • wear in the bearings or joints b. Check car's structure within 30cm of the mounting point for an anti-roll bar for • fractures • excessive corrosion • distortion

IN FRONT

Norwich Union is the market leader for private car insurance. And for commercial vehicles. And motorcycles. Not surprisingly it's become the UK's number one motor insurer. Shouldn't you ask yourself why?

NORWICH UNION

Whatever you drive Norwich Union has a policy for you. High performance and high value cars. Kit cars and modified cars. Even American cars. They can all be insured on Norwich Union's standard private car policy. If you're retired, Motoring Gold is a low cost alternative that rewards experience. And the Collectors Car Policy is specially designed for the low mileage needs of classic cars. If your car is damaged Norwich Union has appointed nearly one thousand Select Repairers nationwide to get you back on the road quickly. And our extensive branch network guarantees a local service. So important when it comes to settling claims.

Norwich Union. Getting alongside customers by identifying their needs.

BEHIND

Norwich Union, as a caring insurer, offers its customers more than just a first class service. Other activities reflect its concern for road safety. Like sponsoring the Highway Code and Driving videos. And the popular Norwich Union Safe Driver of the Year competition. Even the sponsorship of this booklet!
Norwich Union. Committed to road safety and behind you all the way.

SUSPENSION ASSEMBLIES - 12

Is your car's suspension assembly in good condition ?

MAIN REASONS FOR FAILURE	REMARKS	ACTION	✓
1. An anti-roll bar • fractured • distorted • excessively corroded	⚠️⚠️⚠️	Replace	
2. A serious deterioration of bonding or flexible material of an anti-roll bar joint or bearing	⚠️ ⚠️	Repair/Replace	
3. The loadbearing member and/or panel within 30cm of the mounting point for an anti-roll bar is • excessively corroded • deformed • fractured	⚠️ ⚠️	Repair/Replace	

WARNING

 Extremely dangerous. DO NOT drive your car in this condition. You will be breaking the law and risking your life and the lives of others.

 Very dangerous and may be illegal. Put right immediately.

SHOCK ABSORBERS - 1

Are your shock absorbers working properly ?

WHAT THE MOT REQUIRES	HOW TO CHECK YOUR SHOCK ABSORBERS
The shock absorbers The condition of the SHOCK ABSORBERS must not cause danger to any person in the car or on the road The SHOCK ABSORBERS must be in good and efficient working order and be correctly adjusted	a. Check for presence of shock absorbers b. Check each shock absorber for • damage • fluid leaks • insecurity **Note 1** Make sure any leak is from the unit and not from another source **Note 2** Where flexible dust shields are fitted, squeeze shield and watch for a fluid leak under it c. Push down and release each corner of car. Check if shock absorbers are damping effectively **Note** A rough measure of effective damping is if corner of car bounces not more than one and a half times when pushed down and released

SHOCK ABSORBERS - 2

Are your shock absorbers working properly ?

MAIN REASONS FOR FAILURE	REMARKS	ACTION	✓
1. Extensive fluid leakage indicating failed seal	⚠ ⚠	Replace	
2. A shock absorber • badly damaged • corroded • insecure • missing • not producing damping effect	⚠ ⚠	Tighten/Adjust Replace	
3. A shock absorber lever or link is insecurely attached	⚠ ⚠	Tighten	

WARNING

 Very dangerous and may be illegal. Put right immediately.

BRAKES - 1

WHAT THE MOT REQUIRES	HOW TO CHECK YOUR PARKING BRAKE
The brake controls **The parking brake** The condition of the PARKING BRAKE must not cause danger to any person in the car or on the road The PARKING BRAKE must be in good and efficient working order and be correctly adjusted	a. While parking brake lever is being operated, check that at least two wheels are prevented from turning b. Move lever sideways to check for wear in pivot bearing c. Apply parking brake and check that it can be set in the 'on' position and will stay 'on' even when tapped d. Check mountings, structure and panelling for • security • condition

Does your parking brake work properly ?

MAIN REASONS FOR FAILURE	REMARKS	ACTION	✓
1. The car does not have required parking brake system	⚠ ⚠ ⚠	Replace	
2. With reasonable force, lever cannot be set in 'on' position	⚠ ⚠ ⚠	Repair/Replace	
3. Lever releases with slight sideways movement or accidental contact	⚠ ⚠ ⚠	Repair/Replace	
4. Parking brake mechanism not securely attached to car	⚠ ⚠ ⚠	Repair/Replace	
5. Loadbearing member and/or panel within 30cm of mounting point for handbrake is • corroded • fractured • distorted	⚠ ⚠ ⚠	Repair/Replace	
6. The amount of pull before parking brake comes 'on' is more than normal for that type	⚠	Check wear/ Adjust	

WARNING

 Extremely dangerous. DO NOT drive your car in this condition.
You will be breaking the law and risking your life and the lives of others.

 Could also be dangerous and illegal.

BRAKES - 3

Is your footbrake working properly ?

WHAT THE MOT REQUIRES	HOW TO CHECK YOUR FOOTBRAKES
The brake controls **The footbrake** The condition of the FOOTBRAKE must not cause danger to any person in the car or on the road The FOOTBRAKE must be in good and efficient working order and be correctly adjusted	From driving seat a. Check • wear of pedal • part of pedal missing b. Press pedal slowly until pressure can be held Check for creep* Press pedal quickly until pressure can be held Check again for creep

* 'Creep': under constant pressure, a pedal moves slowly indicating an internal or external leak in the system.

46

Is your footbrake working properly ?

MAIN REASONS FOR FAILURE	REMARKS	ACTION	✓
1. The footbrake does not work	⚠ ⚠ ⚠	Repair/Replace	
2. Pedal has inadequate travel reserve	⚠ ⚠ ⚠	Check wear/ Adjust	
3. With sustained pressure, pedal creeps	⚠ ⚠ ⚠	Repair/Replace	
4. Pedal movement is spongy*	⚠ ⚠ ⚠	Replace	
5. Obvious leak in master cylinder	⚠ ⚠ ⚠	Repair/Replace	

WARNING

 Extremely dangerous. DO NOT drive your car in this condition.
You will be breaking the law and risking your life and the lives of others.

* 'Spongy': easy to compress (not hard or solid). If there is air in the system, the brakes will feel 'spongy' when applied, and there may be too much travel (distance between the resting position of the brake pedal and the point where the brakes apply when the pedal is pressed).

BRAKES - 5

Does the brake system work properly ?

WHAT THE MOT REQUIRES	HOW TO CHECK YOUR BRAKES
The braking system The condition of the BRAKES must not cause danger to any person in the car or on the road The BRAKES must be in good and efficient working order and be correctly adjusted	**Parking brake mechanism (under vehicle)** a. Examine all the mechanical parts you can see, without dismantling. Get a friend to keep putting brakes on and off while you check for • corrosion • insecurity • cracking • restrictions to free movement • abnormal movement • too much wear • incorrect adjustment • secure holding on mechanism b. Check • lever pivots • cables • rods • linkages • outer casings • guides • clevis pins • yokes • locking devices

Does the brake system work properly ?

MAIN REASONS FOR FAILURE	REMARKS	ACTION	✓
1. Serious weakening of any component due to • cracking • too much wear • damage	⚠ ⚠ ⚠	Replace	
2. A corroded cable	⚠	Replace	
3. A knotted cable	⚠ ⚠	Replace	
4. A frayed cable	⚠ ⚠ ⚠	Replace	
5. A cable outer casing is damaged	⚠ ⚠	Repair/Replace	
6. Holding-on mechanism is badly worn	⚠ ⚠ ⚠	Repair/Replace	
7. A parking brake lever attachment is insecure	⚠ ⚠	Tighten Repair/Replace	
8. Any restriction to free movement of system	⚠ ⚠	Repair	
9. Unusual movement indicating bad adjustment or too much wear	⚠ ⚠	Adjust/Replace	
10. The loadbearing member and/or panel within 30cm of the mounting point for the parking brake lever attachment is • excessively corroded • deformed • fractured	⚠ ⚠ ⚠	Repair/Replace	

WARNING

⚠ ⚠ ⚠   Extremely dangerous. DO NOT drive your car in this condition. You will be breaking the law and risking your life and the lives of others.

⚠ ⚠   Very dangerous and may be illegal. Put right immediately.

⚠   Could also be dangerous and illegal.

BRAKES - 7

Does the brake system work properly ?

WHAT THE MOT REQUIRES	HOW TO CHECK YOUR BRAKES
The footbrake system The condition of the BRAKES must not cause danger to any person in the car or on the road The BRAKES must be in good and efficient working order and be correctly adjusted	**Hydraulic brake components** a. Check hydraulic reservoirs and cylinders for • security of mounting • damage • leaks b. Check all visible brake pipes and flexible hoses for • chafing • corrosion • damage • security • fouling • leaks • kinking • stretching c. Check for • excessive corrosion at master cylinder mounting • insecure brake back plate or disc caliper housing • vacuum servo not working (see Note) d. Get a friend to apply brakes firmly while you check for • leaks • bulges in hoses **Note** To check vacuum servo 1.With engine switched off, press brake pedal several times to deplete all stored vacuum in servo 2. Hold brake on firmly with left foot and start engine 3. If servo is working, brake pedal will travel further as vacuum builds up in system

Does the brake system work properly ?

MAIN REASONS FOR FAILURE	REMARKS	ACTION	✓
1. A reservoir or master cylinder • insecurely mounted • damaged	⚠ ⚠ ⚠	Repair/Replace	
2. Leak of hydraulic fluid	⚠ ⚠ ⚠	Repair/Replace	
3. Pipes • kinked • chafed • corroded • damaged • cracked • inadequately supported • likely to hinder or be trapped by moving parts	⚠ ⚠ ⚠	Repair/Replace	
4. Hoses • twisted • damaged • chafed • deteriorated • cracked • bulging under pressure • stretched by steering or suspension • likely to hinder or be trapped by moving parts	⚠ ⚠ ⚠	Replace	
5. Vacuum servo not working	⚠ ⚠	Repair/Replace	
6. Insecure or corroded brake back plate or disc caliper housing	⚠ ⚠ ⚠	Repair	
7. A disc or drum is fractured or • excessively pitted • scored • worn	⚠ ⚠ ⚠ ⚠ ⚠	Replace Repair/Replace	
8. The loadbearing member and/or panel within 30cm of the mounting point for the master cylinder is • corroded • fractured • distorted	⚠ ⚠ ⚠	Repair/Replace	

WARNING

 Extremely dangerous. DO NOT drive your car in this condition.
You will be breaking the law and risking your life and the lives of others.

 Very dangerous and may be illegal. Put right immediately.

BRAKES - 9

Are your brakes working correctly ?

WHAT THE MOT REQUIRES	HOW TO CHECK YOUR BRAKES
The braking systems The condition of the BRAKES must not cause danger to any person in the car or on the road The BRAKES must be in good and efficient working order and be correctly adjusted	**Brake performance test** 1. The road • Choose a quiet, level road • Avoid residential streets or causing nuisance • Make sure no traffic is coming in either direction 2. Drive at 20 mph 3. Press clutch pedal and apply footbrake with constantly increasing pressure Brakes must work • effectively • progressively • without juddering • without fluctuation • without the vehicle deviating or swerving 4. Repeat test using handbrake only, keeping ratchet disengaged (button pressed) all the time **To do a more accurate test** 1. Select marker on road (road sign, tree, etc.) Drive at 20 mph 2. As car front passes marker, begin to apply brakes (as above) 3. When car has stopped, step out distance from marker to front of car. Count each stride as a metre. To find out your brake efficiency, see table on left.

Brake Efficiency Table

Effiicency requirement (see page 55)	Metres from marker to car front
50%	8
40%	10
30%	13
25%	16
16%	25

Note. The 'MOT' brake test is more comprehensive. Make sure your brakes are working correctly.

Are your brakes working correctly ?

MAIN REASONS FOR FAILURE	REMARKS	ACTION	✓
1. Brake efficiency is less than required * (see table)	⚠ ⚠ ⚠	Repair/Adjust/ Replace	
2. Brake sticks or binds**	⚠ ⚠ ⚠	Repair/Adjust/ Replace	
3. Brake effort fluctuates when brakes are steadily applied	⚠ ⚠	Repair/Adjust/ Replace	
4. Severe grab or judder when brakes are applied	⚠ ⚠ ⚠	Repair/Adjust/ Replace	
5. Braking causes pulling or swerving to one side	⚠ ⚠ ⚠	Repair/Adjust/ Replace	

WARNING

 Extremely dangerous. DO NOT drive your car in this condition.
You will be breaking the law and risking your life and the lives of others.

 Very dangerous and may be illegal. Put right immediately.

* Brake efficiency can only be measured accurately with special equipment.

* * 'Sticking': When the brakes remain on after brake pedal has been released

   'Binding': When there is a braking effect with the brake control released

BRAKES - 11

WHAT THE MOT REQUIRES

Service Brake
Cars first used before 1 Jan 1915 need have only **one** efficient braking system.

All cars first used on or after that date must have'
- an efficient braking system with **two** means of control, or
- **two** efficient braking systems with **separate** means of control, or
- **one** efficient braking system with **one** control, if the system is 'split'.

A split or dual system has two independent braking circuits which are applied by working a single means of control, usually the brake pedal.

To find out whether your car has a split or dual braking system, check the number of hydraulic pipes leading from the master cylinder. A split or dual system normally has two pipes, or two separate master cylinders.

Cars first used on or after 1 Jan 1968 must have **one** means of control of the braking system which acts on **all** wheels.

Secondary Brake
On a split braking system, the secondary brake is normally considered to be one half of that split system.

Where a split system is not employed, the secondary performance must be achieved by
- the second means of control, and/or
- the second braking system, usually the parking brake.

Parking Brake
All cars must have a braking system which can prevent at least two wheels (one for a three-wheel car) from turning when the car is stationary.

The parking brake for all cars first used on or after 1 Jan 1968 must be able, by mechanical means only, to prevent the car from moving on a 1 in 6.25 (16%) slope.

Brake Balance
The braking effort on one front wheel must be at least 75% of the effort on the other front wheel.

Measuring Brake Efficiency
Brake efficiency is usually measured using specialized equipment such as that used by the MOT testing station.

Are your brakes working correctly ?

BRAKE EFFICIENCY — WHAT THE MOT REQUIRES			
Class of Vehicle	**Type of System**	**Service Brake**	**Secondary Brake**
Motor cars first used on or after 1 Jan 1968	**One** means of control applying to **all** wheels	50%	25%
Motor cars • first used before 1 Jan 1968 • having more than 3 wheels	**One** means of control applying to **at least 4 wheels**	50%	25%
Three-wheeled motor cars first used before 1 Jan 1968	**One** means of control applying to **all 3 wheels**	40%	25%
Motor cars • first used before 1 Jan 1968 • not having one means of control applying to at least 4 wheels (or 3 for three-wheeled cars)	**One** braking system with **two** means of control or **Two** brake systems with **separate** means of control	30% from first means of control	25% from second means of control

WHEELS - 1

WHAT THE MOT REQUIRES	HOW TO CHECK YOUR WHEELS
The wheels The condition of ANY WHEEL must not cause danger to any person in the car or on the road The spare wheel is not included in the MOT Test. However, it would be wise to make sure that the condition of the spare wheel complies with requirements. An MOT tester need not remove hub caps, wheel trims, etc	**Wear or damage** a. Check wheels, particularly the bead rim, for • damage • cracks • distortion b. Check the wheels are secure c. If visible, check that securing nuts and studs are not • loose • missing

Are your wheels in good condition ?

MAIN REASONS FOR FAILURE	REMARKS	ACTION	✓
1. A wheel • cracked • distorted • damaged	⚠ ⚠ ⚠	Replace	
2. A badly distorted wheel bead rim	⚠ ⚠ ⚠	Replace	
3. An insecure wheel	⚠ ⚠ ⚠	Tighten/Replace	
4. Loose or missing • wheel nuts • studs • bolts	⚠ ⚠ ⚠	Tighten/Replace	

WARNING

 Extremely dangerous. DO NOT drive your car in this condition.
You will be breaking the law and risking your life and the lives of others.

TYRES - 1

WHAT THE MOT REQUIRES	HOW TO CHECK YOUR TYRES
The tyres The condition of ANY TYRE must not cause danger to any person in the car or on the road **You must not use your car on the road if the tyre on any road wheel is unsuitable** • for the use to which you are putting the car, or • in relation to the tyres on the other wheels The spare wheel is not included in the MOT Test. However, it would be wise to make sure that the tyre on the spare wheel complies with requirements. **Note** The law on tyres may change in early 1991.	**Unsuitable tyres include** • a tyre is a different nominal size or structure from other tyre(s) on same axle • a tyre on a twin wheel is a different nominal size or structure from its twin • radial-ply tyres fitted to front wheels and cross-ply or bias belted tyres fitted to the rear or • bias-belted tyres fitted to the front wheels with cross-ply fitted to the rear Tyre type is written on tyre sidewall as follows Radial tyres • The word 'Radial' appears on the sidewall • The letter 'R' usually appears in the number, for example, 165 R 13 Bias-belted tyres • The words 'Bias-belted' appear on the sidewall

58

Are your tyres suitable ?

MAIN REASONS FOR FAILURE	REMARKS	ACTION	✓
1. Tyre is unsuitable	⚠ ⚠ ⚠	Replace	

WARNING

 Extremely dangerous. DO NOT drive your car in this condition.
You will be breaking the law and risking your life and the lives of others.

TYRES - 3

Are your tyres damaged ?

WHAT THE MOT REQUIRES	HOW TO CHECK YOUR TYRES
You must not use ANY TYRE that	**Look for wear and damage**
1. Has a cut	a. Raise each wheel in turn clear of the ground*
• longer than 25mm, or 10% of the width of the tyre, whichever is greater, and/or	b. Rotate each wheel slowly and check
• deep enough to reach the ply or cord	• seating of each tyre on wheel rim
2. Has a lump, bulge or tear caused by partial separation or failure of its structure	• surface of tyre, for damage/repairs, etc • there is no evidence of fouling of other parts
3. Has any exposed ply or cord	• there is no contact between twin wheels
On a twin-wheeled vehicle, the inner sidewalls of the tyres must not touch while the tyres are correctly inflated (See Fig. 9 below)	c. Stop wheel and check valve stem for
	• cuts or other damage • alignment
Note The law on tyres may change in early 1992.	*This check can also be carried out without raising the wheels, by moving the car to reveal the hidden parts.

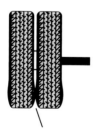

Figure 9. Touching sidewalls
If twin wheels have sidewalls which are making contact ('kissing') with the tyres correctly inflated, your vehicle will fail

Sidewalls 'kissing'

Are your tyres damaged ?

MAIN REASONS FOR FAILURE	REMARKS	ACTION	✓
1. A cut deep enough to reach ply or cord.	⚠⚠⚠	Replace	
2. A lump, bulge or tear caused by failure of tyre structure, such as • separation • tread lifting	⚠⚠⚠	Replace	
3. Any ply or cord exposed	⚠⚠⚠	Replace	
4. A valve stem • out of alignment • damaged	⚠ ⚠	Realign/ Replace if damaged	
5. Twin wheel side walls touching while tyre is correctly inflated	⚠ ⚠	Replace	

WARNING

 Extremely dangerous. DO NOT drive your car in this condition. You will be breaking the law and risking your life and the lives of others.

 Very dangerous and may be illegal. Put right immediately.

TYRES - 5

Are you tyres worn below the legal limit ?

WHAT THE MOT REQUIRES	HOW TO CHECK YOUR TYRES
Tyre tread **ON ANY TYRE either** 1. The grooves on the tread pattern of ALL TYRES must be not less than 1mm deep forming a continuous band at least • THREE QUARTERS of the breadth of the tread, and ALL THE WAY around with visible tread pattern on the remainder **or** 2. Have a depth of at least 1mm, all the way round if the original tread pattern of the tyre did not cover three quarters of the breadth	**Look for wear and damage** a. Raise wheels clear of ground b. Rotate each wheel slowly and check tread wear c. Check that tyre does not have re-cut* tread
Note 1 Re-cut* tyres must not be fitted on cars **Note 2** The law on tyres may change in early 1991.	*'Re-cut' • All or part of the original tread has been cut deeper or burned deeper, or • A different tread has been cut or burned deeper than the original tread

Are you tyres worn below the legal limit ?

MAIN REASONS FOR FAILURE	REMARK	ACTION	✓
1. Tread pattern is not clearly visible over whole tread area	⚠ ⚠	Replace	
2. The grooves of the tread pattern are less than 1mm deep forming a continuous band which is • not 3/4 of the breadth of the tread, and ALL THE WAY around with visible tread pattern on remainder, or • is at least 1mm deep, all the way round if the original tread pattern of tyre did not cover 3/4 of the breadth	⚠ ⚠	Replace	
3. A recut tread (Illegal)	⚠ ⚠ ⚠	Replace	
4. Tyre not correctly seated on wheel rim	⚠ ⚠ ⚠	Refit correctly	
5. Tyre rubbing against • another part of the car • its twin tyre	⚠ ⚠	Repair/ Replace	

WARNING

 Extremely dangerous. DO NOT drive your car in this condition.
You will be breaking the law and risking your life and the lives of others.

 Very dangerous and may be illegal. Put right immediately.

WASHERS/WIPERS - 1

WHAT THE MOT REQUIRES	HOW TO CHECK YOUR WASHERS/WIPERS
The windscreen washers and wipers Your car must be fitted with one or more windscreen wipers with windscreen washers capable of cleaning the windscreen If your car has an opening windscreen there are no requirements There is no requirement on the number of jets in the washers	**Check that car is fitted with the correct washers/wipers** a. Operate windscreen washer mechanism and ensure enough liquid is given out to clean windscreen with the aid of the wipers b. Operate windscreen wipers and check that they move over enough area of the windscreen to give the driver an adequate view of the road in front and forward of the nearside and offside of the car

Are the correct washers/wipers fitted ?

MAIN REASONS FOR FAILURE	REMARKS	ACTION	✓
1. Windscreen washer on driver's side not working	⚠ ⚠	Replace/Repair	
2. Not enough liquid given out to clean windscreen with the help of windscreen wipers	⚠ ⚠	Repair/Replace	
3. A windscreen wiper not working over a large enough area to give the driver an adequate view of the road in front and forward of the nearside and off side of the car	⚠ ⚠	Repair/Replace	
4. A deteriorated blade not working properly	⚠ ⚠	Repair/Replace	

WARNING

 Very dangerous and may be illegal. Put right immediately.

HORN - 1

WHAT THE MOT REQUIRES	HOW TO CHECK YOUR HORN
The horn Your car must be fitted with a HORN which can give audible and sufficient warning of its approach or position The sound must be continuous and uniform, and not strident ONLY SPECIFIED cars (eg. Police, Fire) may be fitted with a ▪ gong ▪ bell ▪ siren ▪ two-tone horn (except as an anti-theft device)	**Check your car is fitted with correct horn** a. Check that horn can be easily sounded b. Operate horn and make sure it gives out correct sound

Is the correct horn fitted ?

MAIN REASONS FOR FAILURE	REMARKS	ACTION	✓
1. No horn or horn control	⚠	Replace	
2. Horn control not accessible to driver	⚠	Repair	
3. Horn does not work	⚠	Repair/Replace	
4. Horn not loud enough	⚠	Repair/Replace	
5. Car fitted with a • gong • bell • siren • two-tone horn	⚠	Repair/Replace	
6. Tone not continuous or uniform	⚠	Repair/Replace	
7. Tone harsh or grating	⚠	Repair/Replace	

WARNING

  Could be dangerous and illegal.

EXHAUST - 1

WHAT THE MOT REQUIRES	HOW TO CHECK YOUR EXHAUST
The exhaust system Your car must be fitted with a SILENCER sufficient to reduce to a reasonable level the noise caused by the escape of the exhaust gases from the engine	**Check that your car is fitted with the correct exhaust** Check exhaust a. is secure and complete b. has no holes c. With engine running, check noise emitted

Is the correct exhaust fitted ?

MAIN REASONS FOR FAILURE	REMARKS	ACTION	✓
1. Any part of exhaust system is missing or in bad condition	⚠ ⚠	Repair/Replace	
2. A major leak	⚠ ⚠	Repair/Replace	
3. Any exhaust mounting • missing • not doing its job	⚠ ⚠	Tighten/Replace	
4. A silencer which is noisy due to being • in bad condition • of a type that gives out excess noise	⚠	Replace	

WARNING

 Very dangerous and may be illegal. Put right immediately.

 Could also be dangerous and illegal.

STRUCTURE - 1

WHAT THE MOT REQUIRES	HOW TO CHECK THE STRUCTURE
The structure The STRUCTURE of your car must be sound and secure and must not cause danger to any person in the car or on the road	Preferably with car over a pit or on a raised hoist, check that there is no • fracture • damage • corrosion on car structure that could adversely affect the correct functioning of a. braking system b. steering gear For the specific areas you need to check, see the diagrams on the following pages

Is the structure of your car safe ?

MAIN REASONS FOR FAILURE	REMARKS	ACTION	✓
1. Any part specified • cracked • damaged • corroded and likely to affect the functioning of steering or brakes		Repair/Replace	

WARNING

 Extremely dangerous. DO NOT drive your car in this condition.
You will be breaking the law and risking your life and the lives of others.

STRUCTURE - 3

Is the structure of your car safe ?

WHAT THE MOT REQUIRES	HOW TO CHECK THE STRUCTURE
The STRUCTURE of your car must be sound and secure and must not cause danger to any person in the car or on the road. The following three diagrams are typical car constructions. The important loadbearing areas are shaded. These must be in good condition.	1. Identify important load-bearing areas 2. Check for corrosion. Press hard and note any 'give' or disintegration. DO NOT • use a sharp instrument • 'dig' at structure • use heavy impact blows 3. 'Bodged' (especially non-metal) repairs may be found by • using a magnet, or • noting dull sound when tapped

SIDE SILL

OUTRIGGER

INTEGRAL LONGITUDINAL SUB-FRAME FRONT TO REAR

GEARBOX CROSSMEMBER

STEERING BOX

Example 1

REAR SUSPENSION MOUNTING AREA

SIDE SILL

FRONT SUSPENSION MOUNTING AREA

SUB-FRAME MOUNTINGS

SIDE SILL

SUB-FRAME MOUNTINGS

STEERING RACK MOUNTING AREA

INNER RIB

Example 2

REAR SUB-FRAME

SIDE SILL

FRONT SUB-FRAME

Is the structure of your car safe ?

Topside of typical car
body of monocoque
construction

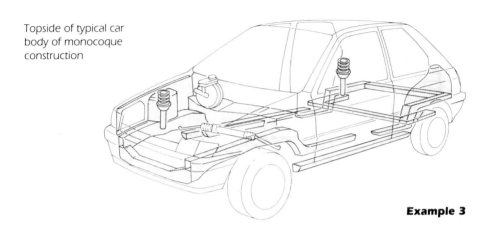

Example 3

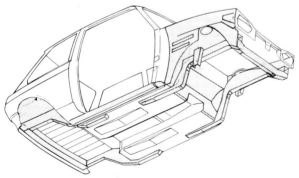

Underside of typical
car body of monocoque
construction. (Doors and front
wings omitted)

Reproduced by kind permission of
the Motor Industry Repair
Research Centre (M.I.R.R.C)

SEAT BELTS - 1

Are your seat belts safe ?

WHAT THE MOT REQUIRES	HOW TO CHECK YOUR SEAT BELTS
The seat belts Your car must be fitted with a SEAT BELT for • driver's seat • front passenger seat if your vehicle is 1. A three-wheeled car over 408kgs unladen, registered on or after 1 Jan 1965 and constructed after 30 June 1964 2. A three-wheeled car over 254kgs unladen, registered on or after 1 Sept 1970 and built after 1 Mar 1970 3. A car first registered on or after 1 Jan 1965 and built after 30 June 1964 4. A goods vehicle not over 1525kgs unladen, first registered on or after 1 Apr 1967 and built after 1 Sept 1966 If there is more than one passenger seat at the front, the seat furthest from the driver is the obligatory one	a. See that driver's seat and appropriate passenger seat are provided with seat belts of the proper type to constrain the upper part of the body b. Pull each seat belt webbing against its anchorage and see that it • is properly secured • has no cuts • has no deterioration c. Fasten seat belt and try to pull the locked sections apart d. Ensure easy release is possible when required e. Examine condition of attachment and adjustment fitting for • distortion • fracture f. Without dismantling, check condition of the anchorage and structure around it g. If seat belt is of a retracting type, pull webbing and check it is automatically wound into retracting unit

Are your seat belts safe ?

MAIN REASONS FOR FAILURE	REMARKS	ACTION	✓
1. The correct seat belt is not fitted to the required seats	⚠ ⚠	Replace	
2. An insecure seat belt	⚠ ⚠	Repair/Replace	
3. For integral seat belts an insecure seat	⚠ ⚠	Tighten/Replace	
4. The webbing is • cut • seriously deteriorated	⚠ ⚠	Replace	
5. A locking mechanism does not • lock • release	⚠ ⚠	Replace	
6. An attachment or adjustment fitting is • fractured • badly deteriorated	⚠ ⚠	Replace	
7. The loadbearing member and/or panel within 30cm of the anchoring of the seat belt is • excessively corroded • deformed • fractured	⚠ ⚠	Repair/Replace	
8. The retracting mechanism does not wind at all	⚠ ⚠	Replace	

WARNING

⚠ ⚠ Very dangerous and may be illegal. Put right immediately.

IF YOUR CAR FAILS

If your car has failed the test,
please read these notes

1. Your car does not meet the legal requirements. If you intend to continue to use it on the road, you should have it repaired WITHOUT DELAY.

2. You will be committing an offence if you use the car on the road if it does not have a current test certificate, except when

- it is not of a testable age, or when you are
- taking it to a testing station for a test BOOKED IN ADVANCE
- bringing it away from a testing station after it has failed the test
- taking it to (or from) a place where by PREVIOUS ARRANGEMENT repairs are to be done to remedy the defects for which the car was failed.

Even in these circumstances, you can still be prosecuted if your car is not road-worthy under the various regulations affecting its construction and use. Also, the insurance may not cover you to drive the car.

HOW TO APPEAL

If your car fails its MOT Test, you may if you wish appeal to the Vehicle Inspectorate's local District Office using form VT17. MOT Testing stations must give you the address of the office and copies of the form.

You must pay a fee which you get back if your appeal succeeds. The completed form (the notice of appeal) and the fee must be received by the Vehicle Inspectorate's District Office within 14 days of the test.

DO NOT repair or alter the items which are the subject of your appeal before the Inspectorate has examined them. If you do repair or alter them the outcome of the appeal may be affected.

Printed in the United Kingdom for HMSO
Dd 292737   C100   9/90